UMOJA MEANS UNITY

An Introduction to the Philosophy and
Programs of Umoja Nation, Inc.

Lost Word Publishing

Umoja Means Unity: An Introduction To The Philosophy and Programs of Umoja Nation, Inc.

ISBN: 978-1-7342202-5-4

Lost Word Publishing

P.O. Box 7828

Richmond, VA 23231

(804) 220-0650

www.lostwordpublishing.com

UMOJA (oo-mo-ja) n. Swahili word for "unity" [as part of the Nguzo Saba (Seven Principles), as developed by Maulana Karenga] meaning, "To strive for and maintain unity in the family, community, nation and race." UNITY implies the oneness, as in spirit, aims, interests, feelings, etc., of that which is made up of diverse elements or individuals; Unity, the quality of being one in spirit, sentiment, purpose, etc.; oneness

NATION (n.) 1. a stable, historically developed community of people with a territory, economic life, distinctive culture and language in common. 2. the people of a territory united under a single government; country; state

"Not 'unity just for unity,' but unity for great achievements, not one of which can be realized without it." -- Chancellor Williams, THE DESTRUCTION OF BLACK CIVILIZATION

TABLE OF CONTENTS

MISSION & PURPOSE

Umoja Nation is established to facilitate cooperation among the various groups, movements, organizations, businesses and individual efforts existing within the Black people of the United States and all over the planet Earth.

Our aims include (but are not limited to):

--the establishment of an independent political party;

--the establishment of an independent educational system;

--the acquisition of land and property to be used for national development;

--the abolition of the prison-industrial complex; and

--the implementation of a strategic economic plan to utilize Black dollars to solve Black problems.

We believe that these aims will be best reached by achieving **NATIONAL CONSCIOUSNESS, COMMUNITY CONTROL** and **PEACE** among our people. These, subsequently, will be developed by utilizing the Nguzo Saba (Seven Principles) of *Unity, Self-Determination, Cooperative Economics, Collective Work and Responsibility, Purpose, Creativity, and Faith* as our foundation and guide.

We know that with *unity of identity* (who we are), *unity of aims* (what we want), and *unity of agenda* (how to achieve it), we can secure a better future for our children and generations to come.

What We Will Achieve[1]

NATIONAL CONSCIOUSNESS is the consciousness of our origin in the world, which is divine. As a people, we were the first in existence and all others derived from us. National Consciousness is the awareness of the unique history and culture of Black people and the unequaled contributions we have made to world civilization. National Consciousness is the awareness that we are all one people, regardless of our geographical origin and that we must work and struggle as one if we are to liberate ourselves from the domination of outside forces and bring into existence a Universal Government of Love, Peace and Happiness for all our people.

COMMUNITY CONTROL is the control of our educational, economic, political, media, recreational and health institutions in our communities. Our demand for Community Control grows from the recognition that the institutions and resources of a community should be structured to serve the members of that community, who are fully capable of deciding for themselves what they need and how to get it. It is prerequisite to our survival that we take control of the life-sustaining goods and services that every community needs in order to maintain and advance itself and advance civilization.

PEACE is the opposite of chaos and confusion and the opposite of confusion is order. Our universe rests on a foundation of Law and Order. Our peace will come as a result of being in harmony with this Universal law and order in all that we do. Peace is the recognition of oneness and the result of unity. We will achieve peace in ourselves, our communities and in our nation. This is our ultimate goal.

THE NGUZO SABA (The Seven Principles)

Our Foundation and Guide[2]

UMOJA (Unity). To strive for and maintain unity in the family, community, nation and race.

KUJICHAGULIA (Self-Determination). To define ourselves, name ourselves, create for ourselves and speak for ourselves.

UJIMA (Collective Work and Responsibility). To build and maintain our community together and to make our brothers and sisters problems our problems and to solve them together.

UJAMAA (Cooperative Economics). To build and maintain our own stores, shops and other businesses and to profit from them together.

NIA (Purpose). To make our collective vocation the building and developing of our community in order to restore our people to their traditional greatness.

KUUMBA (Creativity). To always do as much as we can, in the way that we can, in order to leave our community more beautiful and beneficial than we inherited it.

IMANI (Faith). To believe with all of our heart in our people, our parents, our teachers, our leaders and the righteousness and victory of our struggle.

A foundation is the base on which a thing rests or the fundamental principle on which a thing or idea is erected. It is with this understanding that we take the NGUZO SABA as our foundation. We accept that these seven basic principles are instrumental to the building of a Black nation and if they are not laid true then all our work will be in vain, for whatever we have built will eventually crumble with the movements and pressures of time.

A guide is a thing which gives direction; it is what leads, manages and arranges one's steps so that they take them where they want to go. The NGUZO SABA is not only our foundation but it must be our guide, reminding us of how we want to live, where we want to go and how to get there.

"UMOJA MEANS UNITY"

Umoja Nation works to bring together the various institutions and movements within the Black community in an effort to address our issues through strategic planning and coordinated action. We do not believe in waiting on the benevolence of a racist power structure to give us what we can get for ourselves. We have lost too much time and too many lives attempting to use moralistic arguments to persuade an immoral society. As the great Marcus Garvey once said, "Power is the only argument that satisfies man", and it is in our unity where our true power lies.

This unity must begin with a unified consciousness; a consciousness that perceives us as the same people with the same goals. We cannot continue to allow the illusion of American individualism to cripple us. Every other group of people in this country have the sense to see that solidarity, cooperation and group self-reliance are the keys to advancement and power in America. Now our group must realize the same.

Black people must put Black people first. We are living in an age that demands our unity and if we fail to give to this age what it demands, it guarantees our death. From Trayvon

Martin to Breonna Taylor, and from Ahmaud Aubrey to George Floyd; every innocent black life lost is our call to unite. Our brothers and sisters suffering in penal institutions demand our unity. The underfunded and neglected schools filling our neighborhoods demand our unity. The impoverished and unemployed demand our unity. Our distrust of the medical establishment demands our unity; and not just a momentary unity but, a unity that is enduring and operational, on an institutional, cultural and economical level. This is what we refer to as our *unity for power*.

When we say *unity for power* it means we know that our group's division is a weakness and it is this weakness that holds open the door for our oppressors to walk through. It is our division that creates the opportunity for us to be taken advantage of, manipulated and fleeced like sheep. Internally, we are divided by age, class, religion, politics, gender, complexion, neighborhood and tribe. But these divisions are exaggerated and manipulated to keep us apart. In reality even our oppressors are aware that we are all Black, and it is because of our *blackness* that they equally oppress us all.

Malcolm X once said that the Black man isn't lynched because he is a Christian or a Muslim, he's lynched because he's Black and this age is no different. Black men of all ages, religions and classes are being harassed, assaulted, incarcerated and even killed due to America's irrational response to their *blackness*. We can no longer deny this truth. There is no salvation in our intragroup division. It is only through unity, collective action, cooperative economics and mutual responsibility that we will ever attain true peace.

A unified consciousness is key. If we do not develop a unified perception of who we are, what we want and how we will get it then we will be like a body with three heads. Each head will be leading us in a different direction, and all the while the body will be going nowhere. The founders of Umoja Nation do not presume to know all of the answers. But we do know that we have the ability to figure the answers out, together. Our communities are filled with qualified people in every field of activity. If we work together, we are more than capable of solving our own problems. Therefore, one of our first goals is to hold an Umoja Forum to bring local leaders, business owners and community members together to discuss community issues and to assess what each member has to offer as potential solutions. The purpose of this forum is not just to bring about a list of the community's most pressing issues but also to enlist and engage community institutions and organize its residents in a strategically coordinated plan of action that will resolve these issues.

A commitment to each other and to the attainment of this goal is all we need. We must move beyond our pride, egos and pleas for recognition, and sincerely commit ourselves to our people's advancement. I recall the old African proverb, "I am because we are, and we are because I am." The strength of the group lies in each individual and each individual is made stronger by the group. We must reclaim this mindset.

It is only when Black people begin to put Black people first; when we move beyond our fearful desire to assimilate and integrate into this society; when we heal the inferiority complex and Stockholm Syndrome we suffer from; when we stop trying to prove ourselves and just BE ourselves, fully and without apology; that we will develop the self-love required for a people to stand on their own and define the world according to their interests.

In Umoja we stand and in Umoja we trust.

P.E.A.C.E.

Positive Energy And Constant Elevation
--Saint Sincere (10/22/2020)

"Umoja Means Unity" (pt2)

It has become clear to Saint Sincere and I that now is the time for all Black nationalist groups to set aside their ideological, theological and petty differences. The time has come for us all to unite!

Umoja means unity, and it's my opinion that every Black nationalist movement has been able to accomplish a lot on their own. But it is 2022, its been 403 years since the first Black slave was brought to the shores of the Virginia colony, and sadly, Black people are no closer to freedom than we were 100 years ago. Black earning power is just pennies on the White man's dollar. Black men are still being lynched by White men. Black children are still disproportionately attending inadequate and underfunded schools, and Blacks are still being systematically denied access to resources and funding such as loans and housing.

Each Black nationalist movement has grown to become a mature and independent movement. They all have an established cultural identity that makes them uniquely different from all others and I think this is important, because it means that we each bring something different to the table.

But for those who watch sports, there's a new trend going on right now in the NBA and NFL. In today's league, it's common for multiple All-Stars to join forces to form a superteam. It happened in Boston when Ray Allen and Kevin Garnett joined Paul Pierce. It happened again in Miami when Lebron James and Chris Bosh joined Dwayne Wade. It happened again in Cleveland when Lebron and Kevin Love joined Kyrie Irving. Then it happened in Oakland when Kevin Durant joined Stephen Curry and Klay Thompson. It just happened when Anthony Davis joined the Lakers to play with Lebron James in L.A.. It happened in the NFL when Gronkowski and Antonio Brown joined Tom Brady in Tampa Bay. And it happened again when Von Miller, and Odell Beckham, Jr. joined Matthew Stafford in L.A. There has been a new paradigm shift in the sports world. We are living in an age where the blueprint for winning an NBA title or NFL title now depends on how many All-Star players you can convince to come and join your team.

What would happen if we applied this same tactic in our efforts to fight for Black liberation? What would happen if multiple Black nationalist movements joined forces to form one superteam? Would we then be able to finally take the title away from White supremacy? It will depend on how well we work together, because the NBA also provides us with examples of how important teamwork is when you're part of a superteam. Look at what happened when Allen Iverson joined the Denver Nuggets to play with Carmelo Anthony, Kenyan Martin, and Chauncey Billups? Then there was Russell Westbrook joining the Houston Rockets to play alongside James Harden. There also was the Clippers' failure to live up to their hype when Kwawhi Leonard and Paul George linked up to join forces with Lou Williams in L.A.

Umoja Nation is not a competitor of any Black nationalist movement. It is the unifier of Black nationalist movements. Umoja Nation was formed for the purpose of making a Black nationalist superteam, and I am convinced that if we all join forces and if we work together, this team will be so talented, and our depth chart will be so deep, that not even White supremacy could compete with us. By forming this superteam we can all make our leaders proud and fulfill their visions by finally winning liberation for Blacks which would be the equivalent of making us the new world champions. Individually each group is an All-Star in their own right. We each have a unique talent and possess specific skill sets that are important. But isolating ourselves and viewing other Black nationalist groups as competitors has only served to benefit those who play and cheer for White supremacy to continue dominating the world. None of these groups will have to change their cultural identity to join and the bylaws have been structured around the things we all agree on, and things we unanimously disagree on have been prohibited. The table has been set and the door is now open to any group who wishes to join us. All you have to do is take your rightful seat at the table so that our work may finally begin.

Peace!

--Lord Serious (2/21/2021) revised (4/16/22)

"The Umoja Mentality"

A nation is only as strong as the individuals that constitute it and yet it is the collective nation that further strengthens each individual. Therefore, the members of Umoja Nation should strive to develop a mentality that continually looks within, constantly seeking self-development, while also looking without, spurred by a desire to understand how their individuality can best contribute to the whole. Whether an organization or an individual, Umoja Nation members are part of a team, and it is the responsibility of every player on the team to continually prepare themselves to bring their best to the table.

As members of Umoja Nation each of us should work to cleanse our minds of the many miseducations that we've received from this biased and unjust society. We must labor to remove the Willie Lynch Syndrome of self-hatred and divisiveness, in all its forms, and replace this maladaptive programming with the love of self and love of kind. We must respect our minds and bodies and only feed them what is beneficial to life, growth and vitality. Our mentality should be one that sees the beauty in our people and strives to never unjustly harm any Black man, woman or child.

We must never forget that we are truly one people and that ours is a global struggle against White Supremacy, wherever it stands. However, wisdom dictates that one must first organize their own affairs before they can be of any true help to another. Therefore, Umoja Nation members should be so committed to the upliftment and advancement of our people that we will willingly offer our talents, creativity, time and all else that we can towards our liberation. Ours is a mentality of cooperation, teamwork, solidarity and collective responsibility. We understand that diversity does not mean division and so everyone does not have to be the same for us to work together. Therefore, where some may seek to downplay or deny the multifaceted genius of our people, our history and our culture, ours is a mentality that takes pride in the totality of our existence and actively opposes any person or idea that suggests we do otherwise.

The Umoja mentality is a mentality of self-determination; one that looks out at the world and defines it in terms beneficial to its own interests and goals. Knowing that we are the Original People of the Earth, we know that just as our ancestors mapped the stars and charted the seas, we too possess that indwelling intelligence needed to decipher the universe and set our own course in life. We are a sovereign people by birthright, with the laws of the universe as our only restraints. Yet, we are a wise, righteous and civilized people, and so we do not waste time trying to fight against these laws; we seek harmony with them. We are descended from the Mothers and Fathers of the greatest civilizations to grace this planet. All that we need we have inside, stirring within us like the thick branches of a mighty oak waiting to rise from the acorn.

As members of Umoja Nation, we must recognize the subtle nature of White Supremacy and the insidious way that it permeates every facet of Western civilization. Thus our mentality should be suspiciously critical of any information that we receive. We must never just accept a thing at face value. Rather we should diligently and thoroughly question everything that is brought to us -- and not for the vain pleasure of intellectual masturbation, but for the purpose of acquiring accurate and practical knowledge that can empower us as a people. Although we should trust in our leadership and teachers to guide us, we must never relinquish our own faculties of reasoning and understanding; we are not blind sheep following a shepherd. Our unity does not derive from romanticism, sentimentality or blind faith; our unity results from the conscious perception of the problems plaguing us as a people, and our agreement that collective action is our best way of solving them.

We are not concerned with moralizing pleas to those who seek to hamper and oppose our liberty. We are not here to turn our enemies into our friends. We are concerned with the acquisition of power and all of our means are directed to this end. We are thinkers who think for power, workers who work for power, builders who build for power, teachers who teach for power, preachers who preach for power and warriors who fight for power. We are seeking to empower ourselves, our families, our communities, nation and race and we use the Seven Principles as our foundation and guide.

In our quest for unity, we know that we must be patient and compassionate with our people, for we understand the damage that this White Supremacist system has done; and continues to do, to the minds, bodies and souls of our brothers and sisters. Nevertheless, we also realize that the time is now, and the only chosen ones are the ones that choose themselves. Therefore, we are choosing to make a difference in our world. Members of Umoja Nation do not settle for sitting around and complaining about their problems, we would rather discuss and examine our issues and put together plans to solve them. We do not stop at making people aware of the issues. We work to show them their cause and what we can do about them. We are not lazy, stagnant-minded observers of life; we are hardworking and active participants in life.

We know that just as our ancestors live on through us, we too will live on through future generations and so our work is not just for the moment. We are a forward and far-looking people, utilizing our collective wisdom to put forth progressive plans that advance our interests in the peace, power and protection of our people.

The Umoja mentality is a mentality of oneness, unity and interdependence. It is a holistic mentality in tune with the universal order. It is a mentality that understands that all things matter -- no matter how seemingly small or insignificant -- because all parts contribute to the whole. Thus, the harmonious interworking of these parts is the true aim of the whole, for it is only through this harmony that the whole can ever actualize its maximum potential. As individuals, as families, as a nation and race, this must be our mentality.

In Umoja we stand and in Umoja we trust!

P.E.A.C.E.

Perceive Examine And Critically Evaluate
--Saint Sincere (1/7/2022)

"Black Leadership"

Before we can even determine what is the future of Black leadership, we must first decide what it is that we are fighting for? Because the truth is, not all of us want the same thing. Therefore, there is no way we all want to go in the same direction. But you see this is why leadership is so important. A leader is one who drives the people. It is the leader's responsibility to convince the people that their individual interests would be better served if they all worked together to achieve common goals. So let me tell you a story about Black leadership in America. This is the story of *Martin, Malcolm and Mickey*.

One day Martin Luther King, Jr. and Malcolm X took a trip to visit Mickey Mouse at Disney World. When they walked through the front gates Martin was overjoyed to find Disney characters of all colors happily coexisting in a fully integrated society. When Mickey introduced them to Sleeping Beauty, Martin told her, "I had a dream that one day all Americans would live like this." But Malcolm said, "Even Sleeping Beauty knew that the White Man's dream was the Black Man's nightmare." Next Mickey took them to meet the Black princess, Princess Tiana. Martin sees the progress that Black women have made. They went from being forced to sit on the back of the bus to sitting on a throne. But Malcolm told Princess Tiana that she, "...should be ashamed of herself for letting the White Man parade her around like some token Negro." After that, Mickey presents them to Aladdin and Princess Jasmine. Martin lets the genii out of the bottle while Malcolm greets them in the Arabic word for peace. Lastly, Mickey takes them to see the Lion King. Both Martin and Malcolm are amazed by the majesty of Africa's landscape and wildlife. Mickey informs them that their tour is now over. The two men shake Mickey Mouse's big gloved hand and then they get on a few rides before leaving.

As they're exiting the parking lot Malcolm notices a Black man sitting at the bus stop. "Let's give that brother a ride" Malcolm says. Martin pulls over and asks the stranger if he needs a lift? The man grabs his bag and gets in the back. He thanks them for giving him a ride and then he gives Martin directions to his home. During the ride Martin tells the man all about how he enjoyed his visit with Mickey Mouse. And Malcolm tells the man it's irresponsible for Black leadership to teach our race to believe that America has the potential to become Disney World. Martin then asks the man what he thinks about it. The man replies, "The Black man in America has three choices. He can live like Martin, Malcolm or Mickey. Martin buys into the fantasy, Malcolm sees the fantasy for what it is, and Mickey wears a mask just to blend in."

So when you ask me what's the future of Black leadership, I say it must be authentically Black and sincerely dedicated to speaking truthfully about the unique realities confronting Blacks living in America. I think this form of Black leadership begins on the grassroots level and by virtue of its achievements and successes on a local level, its platform expands regionally and then nationally. This is what substantive future Black leadership looks like. However, there are many people who would rather live a lie; they avoid the truth at all costs. So there are some who prefer the type of Black leadership that promotes the fantasy and gives inspirational speeches to make the oppressed masses feel good. You don't want the harsh truth, you want the feel good lie.

It reminds me of this girl I used to know. She was a real square. If it was fun and exciting she wouldn't do it. You know the type -- A lady in the street and you'll never get her in your bed. Well, I tell you this girl was really in love with me when I was younger. Everytime she saw me she'd get so excited. She'd run up to me and hug me. And once she got a hold of you, it was a world class wrestling match just to break free. So it got to a point where I'd just run away from her or hide from her whenever I saw her coming. Her name was *Truth*. Now *Truth* was a real good girl but back then I was too foolish to appreciate her. I had a thing for this other girl who was so fast her loving came in a paper bag. My mama couldn't stand her either. My mama said, "That girl was nothing but *Trouble*." And the name stuck too. Everyone in our neighborhood called that girl *Trouble*. And *Trouble* flirted with all of the boys in my neighborhood. One day she was my girl then the next day she was yours. She was the real manipulative type who loved to keep drama going. *Trouble* kept all of the boys fighting and beefing over her. But there must be something terribly wrong with us young Black men because for some odd reason, we just couldn't get enough of *Trouble*.

Well it got to a point where *Truth* started coming around more and more. And I found myself running away from her every time she got anywhere near me. But what I never noticed was that every time I ran away from *Truth*, it seemed like *Trouble* was waiting for me. If I was at the gym playing basketball, and I saw *Truth*, I'd run out of the emergency exit and she'd take off after me. And then here comes *Trouble*, helping me escape by hiding me in her house when her parents weren't home. If I was in school walking down the hallway on my way to class and I noticed *Truth*, then suddenly here comes *Trouble* helping me play hooky. It didn't matter where I was at, every time I ran away from *Truth*, I found *Trouble* right around the corner. And I'm not the only one. It's the same for all young Black men living in America. You can go to any detention home, any jail or any prison in America and if you ask the Black boys and Black men how they got there, they will all tell you the same story: I was running away from *Truth* and that's when I ran into *Trouble*.

The problem is that this feel good leadership that would have Black people believe that a brighter day is right around the corner, if we just continue to accommodate our White oppressors are running from *Truth*. And this is why we, as a race of people, are in so much *Trouble* right now in America. Whenever police shoot unarmed Black people and Black leadership gets up on that podium and gives press conferences, taking the stance that if Blacks remain calm and patient justice will prevail, these leaders are running away from the *Truth*. And this is why we keep running into *Trouble* over and over again. When you have Black leadership telling you the key to changing America's race problem is by going to the polls to vote but none of these leaders have taken the initiative to first receive commitments from these candidates, by making them go on record and publicly declare their intentions to pass legislation that will specifically address our group's problems; when these leaders tell you these politicians cannot pass legislation specifically for Black people, but for the past 40 years we've supported them and watched as they've passed bills specifically for the LGBTQ, Asians, Latinos, women and the handicapped; then these leaders are running from *Truth* and they are taking our people on a path that leads straight to *Trouble*.

And you see, these feel good leaders got you fooled. They know their leadership has taken us down the wrong direction. But instead of facing the *Truth* they call the snag they've put us in **Good Trouble**. That's what John Lewis called it, and may peace be upon him, but that's exactly what John Lewis called it and that's what you call it today. I'm very familiar with *Trouble* and that girl knew how to have a *good* time but you always paid for it when you woke up in the morning. **Good Trouble** is what the integrationist calls it. But there's nothing **Good** about *Trouble*. *Truth* is the only thing **Good**. Even Jesus said so. So you see we are not all in one accord as a race of people. You have some Blacks who think *Truth* is **evil** and *Trouble* is **good**. And there are others like myself who've come to understand this kind of thinking is wrong. We were taught incorrectly and we have been miseducated. So Black people today are in dire need of a real political education.

We need to be taught to embrace *Truth* and love her the way she loves us. The future Black leaders we follow must show and prove that they've learned from John Lewis and Martin Luther King, Jr.'s mistakes. Although these men had the best of intentions, they were wrong and they are responsible for misleading Black people when they ran away from *Truth* and took the Civil Rights Movement on a path that led Black people right into the arms of **Good** *Trouble*.

Now the problem dealing with *Trouble* is that whenever she snuck me in her house, her parents always came home before we expected and I'd go through all hell trying to sneak out. Or whenever we skipped school together, it was easy walking out unnoticed but getting the message off of the house answering machine that the school had left before my parents heard it was always a headache. You see, it's easy to get into *Trouble* but it's hard to get out. And my generation is in more *Trouble* than any of the other Black generations that preceded us. The reason is because, unlike those who came before us, my generation is more divided, more selfish, and we are only concerned with competing against each other as individuals. We care nothing about what the Black race must do collectively to become more self-sufficient so that we may learn how to compete against the other racial groups. The whole neighborhood knew that girl was *Trouble* but only the foolish boys who fought over her thought she was worth fighting for. While we were like John Lewis thinking *Trouble* was **Good** the rest of the world knew *Trouble* was **no good**!

Black people want to run from the *Truth* but the *Truth* is the White race will never change. You can convince the White liberal to pass a million laws to protect the Black ballot, and the White conservative will pass a million and one laws to disenfranchise us all over again. Legislators can pass constitutional amendments and civil rights bills but it means absolutely nothing when the judicial branch finds new loopholes to avoid enforcing these laws. This system is rigged and designed to keep Black people trapped in a permanent state of subordination to the White race, and you can run from that *Truth* all you want to but the same *Trouble* that found John Lewis will be waiting for your grandkids 60 years later after you've prevailed in your misguided pursuits.

The White man doesn't want to integrate. He never integrates. When we got something he wants the White man expropriates! He takes it, without fair compensation. If Black neighborhoods are valuable, he gentrifies them. When Black districts become powerful he gerrymanders. The *Truth* is, Black Nationalism and ethnic aggregation are the only real paths leading to racial equality for Black people living in America. But we run away from that *Truth* out of fear. We fear the responsibility of having to stand on our own and take care of ourselves. And we fear what the White race will do to us if Blacks began to collectively compete against White America as a unified group. But by running from this *Truth*, we find ourselves caught up in a trap of perpetual dependency that cripples our family structure. It has destroyed the love and respect that Black men and Black women once shared for each other. By running from that *Truth* we find ourselves being the victims of domestic terrorists wearing badges who shoot us down in the streets, depriving us of our right to a fair trial. While others find themselves spending most of their lives as state property or federal property, while our friends and families must stand helplessly by as they watch history repeating itself.

Today, a new generation of White men have been breaking up Black families. Every time they place their chains and shackles on one of us and they cart us away from our homes, we leave behind weeping Black mothers, Black brothers, Black sisters and Black children. By running from this *Truth*, we have found ourselves in the same exact *Trouble* Black people faced during slavery and Jim Crow. So the *Truth* is, Black people in America have made no substantial progress trying to integrate, and the sooner we accept this *Truth* the quicker we can begin the great work of getting our people out of this *Trouble* we are in.

Today people listen to the lies being told by Trump and Qanon and they ask how could anyone believe this nonsense? But this isn't something new for their race. The Black integrationist and Black accommodationist would have you believe that what you're seeing within the White race is abnormal behavior. But the *Truth* is, this type of behavior is not abnormal for them at all. They did the same thing to justify their enslavement of Black people during the 15th and 16th centuries. They began telling outlandish lies about Black people being inferior subhumans who were soulless, and the same way we know there was no substantial election fraud committed in 2020, the world knew there was no *Truth* to what the White race was saying to justify their enslavement of Black people. But just as we are witnessing the lies being spread by Qanon gain more popularity and traction today, likewise, the lies propagated by those politically united in their support of the enslavement of Blacks underwent this same snowballing effect. In the past these groups of White people eventually gained enough power and influence to rewrite history. This is why the very lies most of the ancient Greek historians would've mocked later became the so-called "common knowledge" that was never questioned by later generations of White Americans during antebellum.

Today we see it is their White extremism that compels them to fabricate lies and storm the capitol building. They even set up gallows to hang the traitors who opposed their overthrow of the government. This behavior is asymmetrical and practically identical to the behavior patterns of past White extremists. Their desire to spread their lies has led them to burn all books and libraries containing knowledge that contradicted their ***alternative facts***. And they labeled the scientist and scholars who opposed them as heretics and many became martyrs after being burned alive. The *Truth* Black leadership cannot continue to run from is that this type of horrific and inhumane behavior, historically, is the typical response displayed by all White civilizations whenever they cannot get their way. And this barbaric behavior has always been tolerated by the White nobility as long as it works to their economic and political advantage. You noticed it was the White corporate elite who forced Trump to make his followers stop. Not one politician had enough power or influence to put an end to the madness that took place on January 6th. It wasn't until the elite White business man felt threatened that they began uniting against Trump and pulling their funding from his businesses that Trump called the whole thing off.

So if these politicians are powerless against the angry White mob. Why does Black leadership continue to instruct us to place our trust in them? This is especially true when considerable thought is given to the fact that none of these politicians, as of yet, have produced one piece of legislation that can deliver racial equality for Black people in America. For these reasons Black leaders cannot continue to buy into the fantasy that America will one day become Disney World.

We need realistic leadership from courageous Black men and Black women. People who will not run from the *Truth* even though it may sometimes scare them. And we need Black leaders who understand the unique situations confronting the Black working poor and Black unemployed, and they must find a way to convince the Black middle class to invest back into Black neighborhoods. We need to teach the Black middle class that by investing in impoverished Black neighborhoods we can all achieve our common goals. We need Black leadership that will educate the working poor and Black underclass that those stimulus checks and government assistance will not last forever.

We are in need of leadership that understands why you put on your mask at work? Why you use your White voice when answering the company phone? Why you smile when you feel like crying? And, why you're cordial and polite when you really want to cuss your boss out? It is the Black underclass and Black working poor who understands that this whole system is a facade. For this class the workplace is just another masquerade. They do what they have to do to make ends meet. They do what they have to do to pay their bills, keep food on their table, a roof over their heads and clothes on their kids' backs. But unlike some of these Civil Rights leaders, they understand that Disney World is just a place to visit. Not even the employee who wears the Mickey Mouse costume gets to live there. As soon as you leave the parking lot, the fantasy ends and reality begins.

--Lord Serious (3/27/2021)

"The Topic of Land"

There are common questions I am often asked: if we are building a nation where are we going to go? Where is this happening? Where is our land? Allow me to address these concerns.

All nations must exist as an idea before they exist in form and this, too, is the nascent or beginning of Umoja Nation, it began in the hearts and minds of the people. If the principles and aims of Umoja Nation do not live in our daily thoughts, actions and beliefs, then Umoja Nation will never truly exist. Regardless of if we own a million acres or just one square foot, this must be remembered. At one point in time Black people controlled the entire known world, yet that control was continuously forfeited, because our people failed to see themselves as a unified nation. Let us not repeat our ancestor's mistakes.

Although a nation is more than a geographical location, space to exercise one's sovereignty is essential to the full development of any people. Therefore, once we have established a nation (or national consciousness) in our internal space -- i.e. our thoughts, beliefs and subsequent actions -- then we move to cyberspace, to umojanation.com. Umojanation.com has been created to serve as the online community for our people. It is here that all those who share the Umoja mentality can put our freedom of expression towards developing solutions to our problems without fear of backlash. It is here that we can pool together our thinkers, builders, scholars and laymen, from all across our various organizations, and begin organizing them in a collective effort to uplift our people. Using Umojanation.com our people can fellowship with like-minded individuals no matter how far apart we may be physically. It is our space to share, to teach, debate, discuss, analyze, critique and evaluate our efforts in gaining true liberation for our people.

By pooling together our ideas, talent and resources in one place, we can then begin to develop a plan to use our collective economic power to acquire land and property. This is a goal that all of our past leaders have stressed and one that we must continue to work towards. When we think of buying land, we should start with farmland and timberland, near fresh water sources, if possible. This will give us the ability to produce food, clothing and shelter for ourselves. Not only making us less reliant on others, but also making us more competitive in the marketplace. If Black people agree that we desire organic non-GMO products or that we want our beef and poultry free range, then why not produce them for ourselves? With farmland, timberland and fresh water we can raise livestock, grow crops and herbs, as well as operate our own fishing, lumber and farming enterprises. A portion of the profits gained from these enterprises can then be invested into developing our community institutions, whether schools, clinics, banks, libraries or what have you. Once we have acquired land, our next goal is to begin acquiring industrial and commercial properties, such as factories, warehouses, storefronts and other buildings that can be used to engage in successful trade and commerce.

But while we are doing this, we must also focus on the areas that we currently inhabit. We must invest our time and dollars back into developing truly functional communities. Too many Black people are living down the street and around the corner from complete strangers. We must re-instill the idea of community in our people. A true community is made up of people who come together in pursuit of their collective interests, not just people who live close to each other. A community cares for and protects its members and their interests. A community has a code of conduct and holds members accountable. A community is full of people who think as *we* and not just *me*. Jim Crow segregation forced us to develop our own communities, and we should never have abandoned them to integrate and live around people who didn't want us next door. This need to be accepted by White people caused us to turn our backs on our businesses and institutions, which subsequently diminished the economic and political power we once generated as a people.

We have to rebuild this sense of community in our people and especially in our youth. Programs like The A.R.M.Y. are essential to instilling a sense of pride and people-hood in our children and the importance of this must not be overlooked. The youth are our future and if we do not instill in them a sense of duty and obligation to their people, when they get older they will eventually leave their neighborhoods behind in pursuit of selfish interests. Honestly, if the community doesn't invest in them, then why would they feel obligated to invest in the community? This is the current situation in too many Black neighborhoods and we must not allow this to continue.

In places where we make up the majority of the population, we should come together to buy up as much of the area as possible. Remember, community control is our aim and ownership is key. Community investment clubs, like the S.O.S. Group program we have devised should be created in every Black area. Collective work and responsibility coupled with cooperative economics are our pathways to power. Programs like the S.O.S. Group can pool together community resources and use them to open small businesses; to give out grants, loans and scholarships; to fund recreational activities and leagues for the children; to fix damaged roads; to build institutions; and to help community members in their times of need. Community control means being self-sufficient as a people and self-sufficiency means becoming competitive in industries where we spend our money. Beauty supply stores in Black communities should be owned by Black people, grocery stores in Black communities should be owned by Black people, boutiques, nail shops, salons, gas stations, restaurants and all other businesses in Black communities should be owned by Black people. And we must support these businesses, knowing that they will circulate their dollars back into our communities, which will help us all grow. This growth then creates the legitimate employment opportunities that lead to reductions in crime and drug abuse. Asians, Middle Easterners and the other ethic groups that set up shop in Black spaces are not members of our community. They do not care about the welfare of our people. They are economic colonizers, taking our wealth and using it to enrich their own. As a community we must not allow this to continue.

We do not have to repatriate or return back to Africa to establish a nation for our people. America is a nation of nations and every functional community that we create is another brick in the building of a strong Black nation on this land. Our people have worked, bled, fought, died and have been buried in this soil -- we have as much of a claim to it as anyone. And if we can see that our young men are willing to fight and die over their neighborhoods and city blocks, rather than chastising them for being warriors, let's work to build the kind of Black communities that we all make can be proud to live and die to protect. Let us look to Black Wall Street in Tulsa, Oklahoma not only as an inspiration but also as a warning. Black community empowerment is possible but it must be protected. If not, it will be destroyed.

Working to build Black communities within America does not mean that we oppose the establishment of an independent and sovereign nation for Black people elsewhere. As we work to build Black communities and acquire land and property to expand them, we also believe that an African continent that is unified economically and politically is in the best interests of all Black people, no matter where they are. Regaining and maintaining control of the Motherland and her resources are key to the peace, power and protection of our people.

Umoja means unity and Umoja Nation seeks to unify Black nationalist groups, businesses and individuals into a movement of allied minds seeking righteousness under Universal Law. What is this Law: that all is one. Therefore, let us all move as one, regardless of location, for wherever Black people come together in the spirit of unity and righteousness, this is where Umoja Nation stands.

P.E.A.C.E.

People Engaged Achieves Community Empowerment
--Saint Sincere (1/15/2022)

"The Need for Nationalism"

Why would we continue to put our hopes and trust into a group of people that have an extensive history of lying to us? This is not 1821; we're living in 2021. Black people today are no longer helpless to change their conditions. Black people today are no longer ignorant and illiterate. Black people today no longer have to try to figure out what we need to do. We don't even have to develop fresh ideas on how to gain independence. The reason is, our ancestors have already paved the path forward for us. And if you are a Black person living in America who has grown tired of the mistreatment our people have received from our oppressors then we must look to the guidance of our ancestors for solutions to solve these problems. What Elijah Muhammad and the Nation of Islam promoted has its roots in the same economic ideology that was taught by the Moorish Science Temple and the Universal Negro Improvement Association. The teachings of Elijah Muhammad may have a unique theological ideology, but it's Black nationalist philosophy was identical to the Black nationalist philosophy that was taught by both Marcus Garvey and Noble Drew Ali. And if we look at the historical achievements made by our race throughout eras in American history it is clear that Black nationalism has consistently demonstrated that it is far more effective than integration. Compare the progress Blacks made under Marcus Garvey's leadership in the 1920s to the stagnation offered by the Civil Rights leadership which put us on the integrationist path to nowhere fast.

Our generation must ask itself, what are our goals? And what strategies will put us in the best position to obtain them? We now know what Black nationalism can do for us. Likewise, we know what integration can do for us. It is Umoja Nation's position that only one philosophy is intended to move us forward as a race of people. Blacks need to ask themselves do they want racial equality or do we just want the White race to take care of us and treat us nicely? Because currently Blacks only earn pennies compared to every dollar the White man earns. Currently Blacks still have the highest rate of unemployment in America. Black nationalism is more effective at increasing Black earning power than integration has ever been. Black nationalism demands Blacks to become business owners and job creators for their own community, while integration has kept Blacks dependent upon the White man to provide jobs and government handouts for Blacks. Black nationalism provides political power and control because Blacks only vote for elected officials who promote and support policies that will positively impact the Black community. Integration keeps us politically powerless and disenfranchised. Using integration, we are the victims of voter suppression and the elected officials we do vote into office consistently betray our loyalty by supporting policies that negatively impact the Black community. Through its programs designed to enforce social re-engineering, Black nationalism has also proven itself as being more capable of fighting the ideology of White supremacy in the psyches of men and within their institutions. The social stratification of America shows that integration, on the other hand, has proven itself as being the perfect philosophy to keep Blacks forever trapped in a subordinate position to all other races. Do not be fooled by the success of the Black elite. They are the exceptions. The truth is, Blacks are the minority in America but it is our race who is disproportionately impoverished. The only legitimate path forward is the path of Black nationalism

--Lord Serious (2/21/2021)

"Message to the Black Capitalist"

Is there a difference between Black capitalism and White capitalism? Capitalism is an economic policy operating on the principle of supply and demand. Anyone can be a capitalist and capitalism isn't necessarily evil. Exploitative capitalism is evil. What is exploitative capitalism? A few examples are whenever companies begin taking advantage of the consumer by monopolizing the industry, exploiting the laborer by withholding adequate wages, and harming the environment by not disposing of pollutants properly. As a result of these forms of exploitation the free market system errodes any government regulation needed to establish balance. While this expression of capitalism is not exclusive to the White race alone, no other group to date has rivaled the White Anglo-Saxons mastery of exploitative capitalism.

However, I don't think much of a distinction exists between White people and Black people as it concerns our belief in capitalism as an economic policy. I think in Western civilizations you have the majority of the population, both Black and White, who are committed to the capitalist system as a means of generating revenue and accumulating wealth. Furthermore, within both groups there's also a minority present who have grown dissatisfied with the disparity and inequality found within this economic system. This aggrieved minority has a tendency to blame the system while completely overlooking the frailty in human nature as being the root of their problems. As long as there is greed and avarice present in humanity, there is the potential for any economic system to be abused and used as a tool of oppression for tyrants, bigots and elitists.

Therefore, where a distinction does exist between Black capitalism and White capitalism, in this country at least, that distinction is distinctly expressed by our respective group's level of participation in the American economy which is determined by our access, or lack of access, to this nation's resources. To put it more frankly, when analyzing the American economy there is a major difference between the level of participation this system permits among the races. In America, capitalism is thought of as being a free market system, open to all who wish to participate in it. But the reality is that although this is true for the White capitalist, these facts have never been applicable to the Black capitalist. The Black capitalist in America has always had his legitimized business ventures subject to overregulation by the White man's government. Some of us who are capitalist bought into the belief that your fortune in this capitalist system will be made or marred by your individual business efforts. If you make the right business decisions and you are a financially responsible person then you can make a fortune and this is true to a certain extent. But then there are others who see the flaws within the American economy and they can see the way capitalism is being used to oppress Black people and they have vowed to try socialism or communism as an alternative. As revolutionary as they think they are – really they are being reactionary, because what they fail to realize is that in those nation's where the workers overthrew the government; those workers shared a common national identity, they had no doubt that the land belonged to them, and they were the ethnic and racial majority. None of this can be applied to the Black man living in America. We have no common national identity. We are all Black but not all of us want to embrace our racial identity. Many of us would switch skin teams at the drop of a hat if we could. Although, we were born in America we are the only group of U.S. citizens who must constantly fight this country for our rights to citizenship. So in reality we aren't really Americans either. We are a lost people with no national identity, who believe we have no rightful claim to this land since we were transported here against our will. And as more and more new immigrants flood this country, and more and more Black women terminate their pregnancies, the Black race is doomed to remain the minority minority in this country. So we cannot compare our unique position to anyone else's in the world. The class struggle of people who were able to successfully use socialism and communism to change their people's conditions does not fit the American model, because this class system is also one based on race.

The American caste system is not a conventional caste system either because it gives the illusion that we all are equally eligible to join any class we choose. But the rules of the game are rigged to ensure that, although all groups will have their own haves and have nots, there will be a disproportionate representation of Black have nots in comparison to all others. Therefore, the Black man in America has no other choice but to learn the rules of the game and stay 10 steps ahead. And the unspoken rule of every economic system is that every economic system is really nothing more than a social system -- it is a system of control that is designed to control the society it operates in. This is true of capitalism, socialism and communism.

Some Blacks would rather quit the game instead of competing, and that's your right. But for members of the Black race who wish to learn how to compete, listen carefully to what I have to say. Today the Black capitalist is a petty nickel and dime hustler when compared to the *cartel boss* in America who is better known as the White capitalist. The White capitalist has a monopoly over most of this nation's industries and his group exercises exclusive control over his nation's resources. The *cartel boss* gives you exclusive access to his compadres while using any means necessary, including terrorism, to deter outside competition. American capitalism is no different than the drug game and in this game, while the Black capitalist only aspires to one day become a kingpin, the White capitalist is born into the privilege of being the descendant of a long line of drug lords.

The *cartel boss* controls the manufacturing and distribution of the product. The Black capitalist in this game is totally dependent upon the White capitalist to supply him with access to the resources he controls, and the Black capitalist cannot participate in this economic system without the *cartel boss* doing so. The Black capitalist does not decide what the fair market value of his products will be. This is determined by the *cartel boss*, who can cut off supply and force prices to skyrocket, or he can flood the market and cause prices to plummet. Likewise, the corner hustler has nothing to sell during droughts and if he wishes to re-up he must pay extremely high prices. When the market is flooded and drugs are plentiful, he must sell *2 for 3s* just to move his product quicker.

American capitalism is just like the drug game. Now I am not condoning drug dealing so please do not misconstrue my intent here. I only wish to explain these complex things using real life examples. So you see the two bit hustler who aspires to become a kingpin has no control over this capitalist system, because he has no control over this industry. This is why he is at the mercy of the *cartel boss*. Likewise, the Black worker who aspires to one day become a business owner is at the mercy of the White elite business man who controls this nation's capitalist system. You cannot graduate from a corner boy to become a kingpin without the *cartel boss* supplying you with product. For this reason the Black man in America cannot graduate from the working class to the middle class without the White capitalist supplying him with access to raw materials and other resources. So this economic system is all about social control. The *cartel boss* needs to control the industry to keep his position of power and the White capitalist is no different. So the problem isn't the economic system. The problem is that the Black capitalist has a very narrow vision of his role within this system.

The Black capitalist has been limited not only by the structural racism inherent within the rules of the game which prefers his group remains predominantly consumers within this economic system. But more shockingly, the Black capitalist has failed to become a producer within this economic system not because he cannot overcome these barriers but because, lacking imagination, their group has accepted their predetermined limited role. The Black capitalist collectively, as a group, does not aspire to become more than a member of the middle class, which I have equated to the rank of a kingpin in this metaphor.

What if the corner hustler stopped desiring to be a kingpin and began playing the game like he had dreams of one day becoming a drug lord? What if instead of operating within the White capitalist system, the Black capitalist had enough balls to build his own?

Now let's divide the Black capitalist into three classes. You have the illegitimate capitalist. They are the poor Blacks who are usually unemployed and/or have completely dropped out of the job market. This group generates their revenue by providing consumers with unlawful goods and services. Then there is the Black working poor. This group works 9 to 5, living check to check. And lastly, there is the Black middle class. This is a class of small business owners and/or Black professionals who have integrated into suburbia. I have purposely chosen to ignore the Black elite because though some may be sympathetic to this economic plan, I prefer to focus on the little people. Now if all three classes of these Black capitalist unified and worked together they have the labor and skills to run and operate their own economy within Black neighborhoods. The only thing they lack are the resources. The first two things we need to acquire are capital and real estate.

However we have access to both of these things. Collectively, these three classes of Black capitalist have enough disposable income to make this a reality. What we see happening in Black neighborhoods around the nation is outsiders have been buying up all of the real estate, both commercial and residential. This restricts our ability to establish an economic foundation in our own neighborhoods, which also undermines our ability to gain political power within these areas. We need the Black middle class to organize themselves and begin competing with these non-Blacks for the right to own the real estate within Black communities. Also, we need the Black illegitimate capitalist to do two things: first, we want them to keep outsiders out and second, we want them to organize the criminal element within these areas to put an end to the unnecessary crime that has been destroying the property value in our neighborhoods. If we can convince the Black illegitimate capitalist to cooperate with the Black middle class and improve our neighborhoods, then more of the Black middle class will be willing to invest their money into rebuilding impoverished Black neighborhoods. Once the commercial real estate within these areas are Black owned then you will begin seeing more Black faces working behind the counter when you go to the corner store, the gas station, the hair store and the nail salon. This is because the Black middle class will hire the Black working class and Black poor, and as we build our communities from the ground up a beautiful thing will start to happen. More Black capitalists will begin to migrate to our area and they will form new businesses to serve unfulfilled needs. So you will see a significant drop in Black unemployment in these areas and with enough time you will also see how this new economic tide raises all ships. As the Black dollar circulates exclusively amongst Blacks within this area, every Black person who participates in this Black economy will see an increase in their personal income.

But what has been happening for the past 50 years is the exact opposite. We have not been protecting our neighborhoods from foreign invasion and outsiders have been coming in, taking advantage of our disorganization and seizing control of our community resources. They see our lack of unity and they have exploited it for their capital gain. They had every right to do this, because it is not their responsibility to teach Blacks how to compete with them. These other groups, whether White Americans or immigrants, understand the importance of group economics. They understand how it can be used to gain social influence and economic and political power. Blacks, on the other hand, have been foolishly placing our individuality above our group and this disorganization on a community level is how we've unknowingly been contributing to the destruction of the Black community from the inside out. Because we bought into the integration myth, we have less Black owned business than we had during segregation. There once was a time when everything in our community was Black owned and now thanks to integration Blacks have chosen to be employees of the White man instead of retaining ownership for themselves.

When the White man decides he has hired enough of us to meet his quota for diversity, the rest of us remain unemployed. These high rates of Black unemployment have a severe social impact on Black neighborhoods and Black households. You begin seeing the morale of the Black poor and Black working class drop and to cope with their depression and anxiety they self-medicate by using drugs and alcohol, which are now in abundance within their neighborhoods because the foreign invader uses it as a tool to destabilize us. They keep us high and drunk out of our minds because as long as we're trying to escape our problems we will never be sober enough to think of ways to solve our problems. As the drug and alcohol abuse increases in these areas, so does the crime. Soon you begin seeing more Black families being evicted, homes being foreclosed, yards left unkept and cars that are left broken down on the side of the road. What was once a wholesome community has now become a run down crime-ridden area, where those who do have talent and skill will leave and never come back the first chance they get. Within the home, the unemployed Black man who cannot provide will not be respected as a man in his own home. And if he cannot find suitable work or if he will not seek new job training, he will either join the ranks of the illegitimate capitalist or he will abandon his family out of shame.

The point that I am making is that the future of Black capitalism is economic nationalism. The Black capitalist of tomorrow will not wait for a job, he will create one and he will not seek to integrate within the White capitalist economic system. Instead, the future Black capitalist will build an all Black economy to rival and compete against America's White dominated economy. The future Black capitalist will not be satisfied with being a soldier in someone else's cartel. The future Black capitalist will not rest until he is El Jefe, the boss who controls his own industry.

-Lord Serious

"Message to the Black Church"

What is the role of the Black church and Black spirituality in the liberation effort? My position is that religious and spiritual propaganda is one of the most powerful tools used to manipulate people into fighting, killing and dying for a cause. Can this work to our advantage in our efforts to liberate Black people? The answer is yes! Of course it can. But what are the moral implications involved in taking this approach? Would this be a corruption of the sacredness of religion and spirituality? Or is Black morality an impediment to the development of a Black nationalist religious ideology and Black spiritual liberation?

First we must recognize that a belief system is an ideology designed to instruct the adherent on how to live a fulfilled life in accordance with the precepts of a doctrine. The sacred writings of spiritual leaders, priests, pontiffs, gurus, rabbis, prophets, apostles, disciples, sheiks and religious scholars are the words that guide the believers' steps to a desired destination in the hereafter. These men and women are believed to speak on behalf of the creator and others are believed to have possessed advanced knowledge and wisdom about the inner workings of life which gave them a certain authority over our everyday human affairs. Some believe these divinely inspired people had the ability to predict things before they occurred and others are believed to have exercised such mastery over the laws of physics that they could command matter and bend it to their will.

In times past, before the advancement of technology, humanity looked to these men and women to inform them of future weather patterns and they asked them to intercede on their behalf to ask their gods to bring rain and to bless them with a good harvest after planting their crops. But today, thanks to Doppler technology and an improved understanding of the science of meteorology, humanity in advanced nations only need to turn to the morning news or look for the weather report on their phone before beginning their morning commute to work.

In addition to this, before making serious decisions the people sought the advice of oracles and prophets, especially before heading out on any dangerous expedition or waging war. They desperately sought signs from the heavens that they could interpret as good omens to comfort their loved ones whom they were leaving behind and to inspire them to muster up the willpower needed to survive the difficult journey that was ahead. In fact during ancient times men like Alexander the Great and Hannibal would promote propaganda that they themselves were the reincarnation of demigods such as Hercules to inspire their soldiers to fight courageously and to command their obedience. Today we see the same manipulation of religious ideology being used to spread propaganda that inspires people to perform terrorist acts in the name of their God. The bigotry of the White Christian nationalist and the Arab Islamic extremist both justify their actions by interpreting their religious scriptures in a way that is sympathetic to the means they use to reach their desired ends.

Now I know this appears to be immoral on all levels but on a closer inspection of the facts you'll discover that although most religions promote morality, its use as a tool to engender public support for committing acts of aggression against the "other" historically has been amoral. There is a difference between being moral, immoral and amoral. When something is moral it is right; when something is immoral it is wrong; and when something is amoral it is indifferent. So although Moses taught the Israelites that their God commanded "Thou shalt not kill", "Thou shalt not covet", and "Thou shall not steal" as moral principles. Moses -- the leader and founder of a nation -- was amoral when it came to killing the Canaanites and taking their land away from them. But from the Canaanite perspective, wouldn't this behavior be considered immoral?

This paradox is found all throughout history and it affects all nations who are adverse to one another. A common saying is "One nation's liberator is another nation's terrorist." So while the religious and spiritual person looks at such things as being immoral, what they fail to realize is that they most likely would not have the luxury of openly practicing their beliefs if it was not for the amoral behavior of the men who founded their religion and/or their national government. One reason for this is because when you are fighting to liberate an oppressed minority group, the laws of the land are usually written by the majority, and those laws are designed to protect the interest of the majority who hold power. Jesus, Prophet Muhammad and George Washington were all considered criminals in the eyes of their opposition's government. American expansionism was fueled by the settlers' belief in Manifest Destiny, which was a belief that America had been ordained by God to expand across the entire North American continent. This manipulation of the word of God justified the otherwise immoral behavior of White Christians against the Native Americans, and the same thing is occurring today. America's War on Terror and its War on Drugs were all political tools used to unite White Anglo-Saxon Christians and Jews against non-Whites who the government wished to criminalize and dominate.

Now that we have recognized how others use their religious and spiritual beliefs to politically unite their people and justify their acts of aggression to seize and keep power, we should perform a brief analysis of how this same principle has been used by Black liberators here in America. One of the most notorious was Nat Turner. Nat Turner was a Black slave preacher in South Hampton, Virginia. He was thought to be a prophet by many of the slaves who made up his congregation and who listened to his sermons. It has been recorded that Nat Turner had visions that he was destined for great things to come and he interpreted an eclipse as a sign from God to organize and lead one of the deadliest slave revolts in America. Nat Turner and his band of rebels killed White men, women and children, sparring none; in the same way Moses of the Bible allowed his God to use him to unleash plagues that inflicted death and suffering on the Egyptian men, women and children. So although murdering children would be viewed as an immoral act to most Christians today, according to Nat Turner and Moses, this behavior was justified by the fact that these very children would one day grow up to become the oppressors of their people.

A more recent example of the Black Church and Black spirituality playing a role in our people's liberation efforts can be found in the Civil Rights era. Black churches were responsible for producing Black leadership who made the fight for equal rights for all people, regardless of race, a national issue. The shortcoming of these leaders is that their vision was too narrow. They thought civil rights would be enough to provide Blacks with racial equality here in America.

However, our focus is on how Black churches and Black spirituality can be used to unify our people and how these vehicles can mobilize Blacks. Whenever Black spiritual leaders develop the consciousness to understand that their spiritual text authorizes them to protect their flock from the political wolf and economic thief, then these good shepherds will use everything in their arsenal to protect their flock and lead them to safety. This means we will see more Black churches and Black spiritual leaders encouraging their membership to become more politically active and more economically responsible. In fact, they will use their scripture as their authority to advocate for these changes and they will use their influence to organize or aid more informed individuals in organizing their congregations.

As we've seen throughout history, religious and spiritual matters have consistently been interpreted to justify political action and social reengineering. Therefore, when it comes to liberating an oppressed group from oppression, history considers these policies to be amoral. They were neither right or wrong, they were just necessary. So what is necessary for our group to thrive here in America? And what can the Black church and Black spirituality do to aid our group in implementing these necessary changes?

First and foremost, we need Black religious and Black spiritual people to study their sacred texts and learn to interpret their divine scriptures as words that authorize and encourage Black empowerment economically, politically and socially. Once Blacks begin to believe that their God is on their side, and supports their efforts to liberate their people from White oppression then this faith can only be shown and proven through their actions. We need the Black church and all Black religious organizations to become more involved in rebuilding Black communities. We need them to open their doors to us, not just for Bible study, choir rehearsals, bake sales and Sunday services; we need them to open their doors and allow grassroots leaders to use their facilities for community programs such as GED and vocational training. We need them to offer day care and night care services to working single parents.

In addition to this, we need our Black churches to organize community events for the youth. They can sponsor organized sports leagues, talent shows, fashion shows and offer music lessons. These programs will expose our children to new experiences and it will keep them involved in positive and constructive activities in a safe environment. We need the Black church to invest in its membership and the surrounding area. Blacks who attend their services should be able to seek financial aid from the Black church in the form of small loans and educational grants, and when property in our neighborhoods is being sold; we need the Black church to buy this residential and commercial real estate and take advantage of these investment opportunities. Then they will be in a position to better serve the financial and social needs of its congregation by starting small businesses that can be run and operated by its membership and employ the residents who live in the area.

If Black churches and Black spiritual leaders would begin taking these steps then I am confident that the Blacks who are directly benefiting from these programs would be inclined to follow the guidance of their spiritual leaders, say, if he or she would endorse a candidate or a particular policy. These spiritual leaders would hold great political power in their community because they could convince their followers to vote as a bloc. As long as they controlled the commercial and residential real estate in their political district and the Black people in this district remained politically united; these Black people would no longer have to march and beg. Why? Because they would have acquired enough power to make demands from local, state and federal elected officials.

But the first step we need the Black church and Black spiritual leaders to do is they must stop teaching Black people that their God wants them to be submissive and subservient to White oppression. We need them to use their sacred texts to teach Black empowerment and to.encourage Blacks to exercise self-determination. If they would meet the requirements of this first threshold then I guarantee Blacks would not continue to accept being subject to such disrespect, abuse and mistreatment. Now the Black church and Black spiritual leader does not have to support violence, but I don't think they should be opposed to it either. I think in areas where the government has a history of failing to protect Black bodies from White oppression then that Black church is well within its rights to take any lawful security measure that its leadership thinks is necessary to protect Black people and their property. Taking such a step is neither moral or immoral, it is just necessary due to the circumstances. Therefore, that makes it amoral. Did not Simon and Levi take up swords against the Hivite men who raped their sister Dinah? Did not Joshua take the city of Jericho by force? Doesn't scripture tell us that it was David who slayed the giant Goliath? And that it was the apostle Paul who had God blind the sorcerer Bar-Jesus? This is just a brief analysis of Biblical accounts where we are instructed that righteous indignation and self-determination justifies the oppressed minority to take justice into their own hands.

--Lord Serious

A Brief Summary of Umoja Nation's Proposed Programs

While Umoja Nation's primary goal is to facilitate cooperation among the various groups, movements, organizations, businesses and individual efforts existing within the Black people of the United States and all over the planet Earth, the organization will also enact its own independent programs to further its goal of Black social, economic and political empowerment. These programs include, but are not limited to, the following:

UMOJA FORUM

An annual gathering of community members, business owners, spiritual leaders, grassroots activists and other invited guests from varying fields of study, focused on analyzing our issues, submitting programs for solving them and coordinating our actions.

S.O.S. GROUP

A community investment and financial literacy program that seeks donations from all the businesses that profit from the community, to be reinvested into developing human potential and funding community building and ownership initiatives. The S.O.S. Group can serve as a community bank that its members have a direct stake in.

MASTER'S ACADEMY

An Afrocentric educational program that promotes race empowerment and cultural pride.

THE A.R.M.Y.

An incentivized activism program for the youth. The program will seek donations from various brands to redistribute as items to be purchased through the currency that participants can gain by engaging in community development, humanitarian and activist activities.

UMOJA NATION APP

An online community for U.N. members and supporters; used to foster dialogue, unity, self-determination, empowerment and resourcefulness amongst the people.

UJAMAA101 APP

A business networking app that seeks to connect disparate Black businesses into a network of interdependent commerce.

IMANI APP

A specialized relationship app for the Afrocentric holistic community that seeks to unite people and foster relationships around the core values and principles that will build strong families and friendships in the Black community.

CHANGE THE NARRATIVE

A prison abolition program that seeks to humanize and politicize the Black incarcerated population through educational material and economic empowerment.

FOR THE CULTURE

An online talk radio show that discusses important issues in the Black community from a nationalist perspective.

T.N.T. PARTY

A political education program that seeks to educate the Black community on the proper methods of, and necessity for, collective civic engagement and coordinated group action.

THE S.O.S. GROUP (Community Economic Development Program): A Brief Outline

SUMMARY

The S.O.S. Group is a community investment and financial literacy program that utilizes donations from the businesses that service the community, along with U.N. membership dues, to invest into developing human potential and funding community building and ownership initiatives in the area it serves. Each regional S.O.S. Group will operate in its specific territory when it comes to local issues but will also coordinate interdependently with other branches in regards to the U.N.'s collective agenda.

ORGANIZATIONAL STRUCTURE

The S.O.S. Group should be structured as follows:

BOARD OF DIRECTORS: The Board of Directors shall consist of 3-5 U.N. Society class members, preferably with backgrounds in finance, education, investing, entrepreneurship and community activism. No members of the Trader class will be allowed to serve on the Board. Board members shall be elected according to the procedure outlined in the bylaws and shall serve for a term of three (3) years. There will be no limit on the amount of times a Board member can be re-elected. The Board will be responsible for the S.O.S. Group's financial responsibilities and investment portfolio. Subsequently, the Board shall have the power to appoint people to any positions necessary to achieve the S.O.S. Group's mission and goals, including (but not limited to): accountants, administrators, fundraising specialists, grant writers, independent contractors and managers.

MEMBERS: All Society class members qualify for participation in the program. Individuals with General class membership must apply for S.O.S. membership, according to the procedure outlined in the bylaws, and be accepted. An additional monthly due of five dollars ($5.00) is required for a member to be eligible to receive any direct benefits from the program, including but not limited to: emergency relief aid, grants, scholarships, loans, and business investments. All S.O.S. Group members are required to comply with the Consumer Loyalty Program, and also attend Financial Literacy class and Conscious Consumer class, as well as meet all other requirements of members as listed in the bylaws. All S.O.S. Group members will have the power to vote for Board members during election periods, submit proposals to the board and have access to the S.O.S. Group's financial records within a reasonable time upon request. All S.O.S. Group members shall have the power to vote on any community investment venture or other activities of the Group requiring a vote.

DONATORS: This group shall consist of businesses that derive their income from the community that the S.O.S. Group serves, who agree to make regular tax deductible donations to the Group, in return for becoming a part of the Consumer Loyalty Program.

S.O.S. PROGRAMS

Conscious Consumer Class: This program should teach members how to shop smarter, including, but not limited to: how and when to barter, bargain hunt, buy wholesale, do-it-yourself, evaluate quality and the importance of spending money with businesses that directly support the community.

Financial Literacy Class: This program should seek to educate members on the basics of money management and wealth creation, including, but not limited to: how to properly use and build credit, budget, bank, pay taxes, save and invest.

Business Start Up: This program should teach the basics of entrepreneurship, including but not limited to: business management, taxes, marketing and sales, business plan development, and accounting. This class is required for any member seeking a business grant or loan from the S.O.S. Group.

Consumer Loyalty Program: Participation in this program is a requirement of all S.O.S. Group members. This program requires members to commit to only spend their money with those businesses who are listed as Donators and to use their collective buying power to remove lecherous businesses from the community. In exchange, participating businesses will offer S.O.S. members incentives, such as members-only discounts or events.

The A.R.M.Y. (Assembly of Revolutionary Minded Youth) Program:
A Brief Outline

SUMMARY

The A.R.M.Y. is a program that utilizes incentives to get young people involved in community development and activist activities. The A.R.M.Y. will seek donations from popular and/or culturally-conscious brands that it can redistribute as items to be "purchased" with the currency A.R.M.Y. members gain through their completion of specific tasks (aka "Change"). Essentially, the program works to encourage community engagement among young people by incentivizing humanitarian projects (i.e., cleaning parks, painting over graffiti, volunteering, mentoring, etc) with the things they desire (i.e., shoes, clothes, toys, video games, movies tickets, concert passes, food coupons, etc.).

ORGANIZATIONAL STRUCTURE

The A.R.M.Y. will be organized into four groups of participants: Captains, Lieutenants, Soldiers and Allies.

CAPTAINS: Only members of the Society class are eligible to hold this position. Captains are responsible for finding and/or creating activities and events (aka "Campaigns") for the A.R.M.Y. to engage in. Captains are also responsible for seeking and obtaining the donations that will be offered to the Soldiers through the A.R.M.Y. Store. Captains are ineligible to receive "Change."

LIEUTENANTS: Only members of the Society class can fill this position. Lieutenants are ineligible to receive "Change." Lieutenants will consist of former Soldiers who have been promoted due to their commitment to the A.R.M.Y. To become a Lieutenant, Soldiers must apply for the promotion and be approved by their local Captains and Lieutenants, in accordance with the procedures outlined in the bylaws. Lieutenants will be responsible for organizing, promoting and managing local Campaigns. Lieutenants will also be responsible for managing "Change" accounts.

SOLDIERS: All members of Umoja Nation are eligible for this position. Soldiers will consist of young men and women who have registered for the program and then have signed up for and completed a Campaign, where they will complete assignments in exchange for "Change." This "Change" can either be saved or exchanged for the items in the A.R.M.Y. Store. Soldiers who are members of the Society class are eligible to become Lieutenants, according to the procedures outlined in the bylaws. Soldiers will be able to receive badges, bonuses, rankings and other extra incentives to reward and encourage frequent participation in the program.

ALLIES: This group consists of the corporations, entertainers, small businesses and all others who donate a product and/or service to be included in the A.R.M.Y. Store in return for promotion and limited inclusion in the Consumer Loyalty Program.

THE A.R.M.Y. STORE[3]

An online store and/or print catalog that displays all of the items available to Soldiers, their quantity and price (in "Change"). Ideally, Soldiers should be able to purchase items from the Store at all times.

OPERATION

The A.R.M.Y. program will operate as follows:

Captains will create and/or find suitable activities that qualify as Campaigns. The Lieutenants will then promote the Campaigns to the Soldiers, including such information as time of Campaign, sign up deadlines and amount of Change rewarded for completion. The Lieutenants will also organize the time and place for all participating Soldiers to meet up, sign in and travel to Campaign sites (vans, buses, and/or other vehicles may be rented for this, as necessary). Food, drink and rest should also be provided as necessary. At the conclusion of the Campaign, Lieutenants will update Soldiers' Change accounts to reflect their completion of the Campaign. Soldiers can then purchase items from the A.R.M.Y. Store once their accounts have been updated. (All of the above is subject to the provisions outlined in the bylaws.)

NOTE

It is preferable that the A.R.M.Y. Store and Soldiers' Change accounts are kept online so that Soldiers can monitor their accounts and purchase items when they desire. Also, a cryptocurrency token could be created to serve as the currency (i.e. a "Change" token) that the A.R.M.Y. utilizes and/or that all Umoja Nation members use when conducting transactions. In the event that this cannot be created, a simple ledger system can be used to monitor each Soldier's amount of Change. If this is to be done then the Lieutenants should set up specific times and places for items to be purchased and accounts updated. All changes to the accounts should be signed off by the Lieutenant overseeing the Campaign and/or Store.

As the A.R.M.Y. program grows, it should develop its own online community where all participants can create personalized profiles and communicate with each other. These profiles should also keep track of their Change accounts and allow them to make purchases from the Store. Until this community is formed, the A.R.M.Y. should operate as a group within the larger Umoja Nation online community.

About The Founders

Umoja Nation was founded on January 30, 2021 as a Virginia Corporation in a desire to aid in the work of uplifting and liberating the Black people in America and all over the planet Earth. Although this particular corporation may have been created by the men whose names appear below, the principles and spirit of Umoja Nation have been coursing through the blood of Black people since we arrived on these shores in chains and shackles. The founders of Umoja Nation are only the continuation of our ancestors' spirit and they hope that this work is able to honor them as much as they deserve. We pay all homage and due praise to those that came before us and all those who continue to stand firm and fight for truth, righteousness and the liberation of our people.

Praising Each Ancestors Contribution Equally
P.E.A.C.E.

Saint Sincere (Hon. Quentin Morgan) is an incarcerated author, activist and entrepreneur serving a 48 year prison sentence for a robbery and murder he committed at 20 years old. In 2012, Saint joined the Nation of Gods and Earths where he was introduced to Black Liberation ideas and the philosophy of Black Nationalism. Since then he has been committed to using the knowledge he's gained to help improve Black communities and provide better opportunities for young Black boys and girls. Whether through his books, businesses or activism Saint continually works to raise Black people into a national consciousness of who we are, what we want and how to get it.

Contact Saint by email: kingquent100@gmail.com or on Instagram @saint_quintessence

Lord Serious (Hon. James Boughton) is an incarcerated activist and author committed to developing the national consciousness of the Black race. In 2006, Lord Serious was incarcerated for murder and while in prison, he was introduced to the Nation of Gods and Earths and their knowledge of self curriculum. Since then, Lord Serious has become a dedicated activist and educator, inspiring many young men to better decision making and higher living inside and outside of prison.

Contact Lord Serious by email:
Lordseriousspeaks@gmail.com or on Instagram
@lordseriousspeaks

To learn more about Umoja Nation you can contact us at:

Umoja Nation, Inc

PO Box 7828

Richmond, VA. 23231

Phone: 804-220-0650

Website: www.umojanation.com

Email: Umojanationworldwide@gmail.com

Facebook: www.facebook.com/Umojanation

Instagram: www.instagram.com/umoja.nation

References

[1] (adopted from "What We Will Achieve" created by Beloved Allah, Allah Mind, Allah Supreme and Shahid M. Allah, members of the Nation of Gods & Earths)

[2] These terms are given as defined by Maulana Karega, creator of Kwanzaa, founder of Us Organization

[3] The A.R.M.Y. Store may grow into a physical location where Soldiers can shop using their Change accounts.